COUNTRIES OF THE WORLD

SPAIN

NEIL CHAMPION

Evans

TITLES IN THE COUNTRIES OF THE WORLD SERIES:

ARGENTINA • AUSTRALIA • BRAZIL • CANADA • CHILE •
CHINA • EGYPT • FRANCE • GERMANY • INDIA • INDONESIA
ITALY • JAPAN • KENYA • MEXICO • NIGERIA • POLAND
RUSSIA • SOUTH KOREA • SPAIN • SWEDEN • UNITED KINGDOM
USA • VIETNAM

Published by Evans Brothers Limited
2A Portman Mansions
Chiltern Street
London W1U 6NR

First published 2006
© copyright Evans Brothers 2006

British Library Cataloguing in Publication Data
Champion, Neil
Spain. – (Countries of the world)
1. Spain – Juvenile literature
I.Title
946'.083

ISBN 0 237 52856 8
13-digit ISBN (from 1 January 2007) 978 0 237 52856 0

Editor: Patience Coster
Designer: Mayer Media Ltd
Picture research: Lynda Lines and Frances Bailey
Map artwork by Peter Bull
Charts and graph artwork by Encompass Graphics Ltd

Produced for Evans Brothers Limited by
Monkey Puzzle Media Limited
Gissing's Farm, Fressingfield
Suffolk IP21 5SH, UK

Picture acknowledgements
All photographs are by Neil Champion, except: Corbis 15 (O.
Alamany and E. Vicens), Getty Images front cover top (John
Lawrence), front cover bottom (Michael Busselle/Stone),
front endpapers (Michele Westmorland/The Image Bank), 11
bottom (Jack Guez/AFP), 21 (José Luis Roca/AFP), 24 (Rafa
Rivas/AFP), 36 (Miguel Riopa/AFP), 39 (Terry Williams/
Photographer's Choice), 47 (Frank Herholdt/Stone), 57 top
(Christophe Simon/AFP); Jon Arnold Images 53 top (Walter
Bibikow); Photolibrary.com 22 (Todd Dacquisto); Reuters 11
top (Marcelo del Pozo), 25 (Gustavo Nacarino); Rex Features
23 top (Alex Segre), 28 (Andrew Drysdale), 30 (SIPA), 37 top
(Alex Segre), 40 (Veronica Garbutt), 41 (Patrick Frilet); Robert
Harding Picture Library front cover upper middle (Gavin
Hellier), 12 (Gavin Hellier); Topfoto.co.uk 26 (Rob
Crandall/The Image Works), 33 top (Ray Roberts); The Travel
Library 13.

Endpapers (front): A view over the city of
Barcelona, Cataluña.
Title page: An employee at a bakery in the
centre of Granada.
Imprint and Contents pages: Horses and kite-
flyers on the beach at Tarifa in southern Spain.
Endpapers (back): Cave houses built into the
soft rock (tufa) of the desert at Guadix.

CONTENTS

The Spanish flag consists of red and yellow bands. Both colours are traditional in Spain, and they originate from the coat of arms of the early Spanish kingdoms.

A view of rural Spain today – a small farm surrounded by olive groves.

Spain is a large country in Western Europe, second only to France in size. It extends approximately 805km north to south and 885km west to east. After Switzerland, it is the highest European country, with an average altitude above sea level of around 600m. The centre of Spain is a large, high plateau called the *Meseta*, in the middle of which is Madrid, at 660m the highest capital in Europe. Spain also includes two very different groups of islands. The Canaries, off the north-west coast of Africa, are volcanic and very hot, with palm trees and banana plantations. In contrast, the Mediterranean Balearic Islands are on the whole much greener and the climate is milder. Spain also has two small enclaves on the North African coast – Melilla (administered from Málaga) and Ceuta (administered from Cádiz).

IBERIA THROUGH HISTORY

The ancient name for Spain is Iberia, and the landmass made up of Spain (85 per cent) and Portugal (15 per cent) is still known as the Iberian Peninsula. Throughout history, invading armies of Romans, Celts and ancient Greeks have left their mark on the Spanish landscape and people. Their legacies range from the Latin base of the Spanish language, the Roman Catholic faith, the Celtic farming patterns, and the physical features of the people themselves. Perhaps most evident is the influence of the Moors, Muslim conquerors from North Africa who arrived in

Spain in AD 711 and quickly seized control of most of the country. They brought with them great scientific ideas, artists and craftspeople, ingenious agricultural methods and new varieties of food. Their heritage includes the terraces and irrigation channels of the Alpujarra (in the foothills of the Sierra Nevada), the stunning architecture of the Moorish capital, Córdoba, and one of the greatest palaces ever built, the Alhambra at Granada.

By the late fifteenth century, Christian armies had defeated the Muslim rulers, after long and bitter wars. In 1492, the country was finally unified under the Catholic Queen

The Alhambra near Granada is one of the finest examples of Moorish architecture in Spain.

Isabella and King Ferdinand. In the same year, Christopher Columbus sailed from the Iberian Peninsula in search of a sea route to India and the Far East. Columbus did not reach Asia, but stumbled instead upon the Bahamas and the American continent. This began the golden age of Spanish history. Explorers to South and Central America brought back wealth in gold and silver, which filled the treasury of the Spanish monarchs. During the sixteenth and seventeenth centuries, Spain became the most powerful nation in Europe and probably the richest on Earth.

KEY DATA

Official Name:	Reino de España (Kingdom of Spain)
Area:	504,750km^2
Population:	40,752,000
Main Cities:	Madrid (capital), Barcelona, Valencia, Zaragoza, Sevilla, Málaga, Bilbao, Las Palmas de Gran Canaria, Murcia, Córdoba, Palma de Mallorca, Granada
GDP Per Capita:	US$22,391*
Currency:	Euro (€)
Exchange Rate:	US$1 = 0.83 Euros £1 = 1.51 Euros

*(2003) Calculated on Purchasing Power Parity basis
Sources: UN; World Bank

MAJOR CITIES AND TOWNS

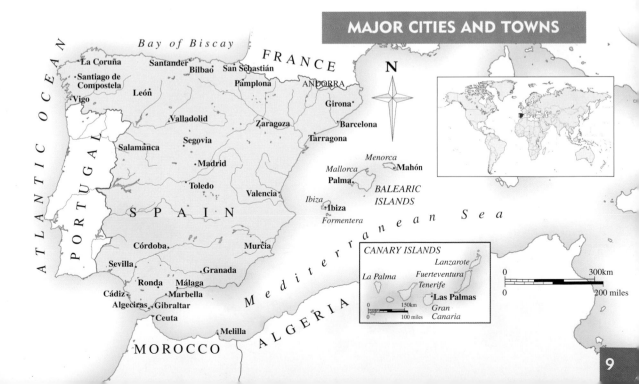

However, war with Protestant countries, including England and the Low Countries, led to a decline in wealth and influence. In the early nineteenth century the French, under Napoleon Bonaparte, invaded Spain but were finally repelled by Spanish and British forces. In the twentieth century Spain became isolated from most of the rest of Europe under General Francisco Franco, a right-wing dictator. With the assistance of two other dictators – Adolf Hitler in Germany and Benito Mussolini in Italy – Franco and his extremist Falangist Party seized power in 1936 after a bitter civil war. He remained in control until his death in 1975. From the 1960s, Spain began to develop economically. Following the end of the Franco regime, this growth was used to help make the country's wealth comparable to its European neighbours.

SPAIN TODAY

Since the mid-1970s, Spain has undergone huge economic growth. More jobs and better pay for most of its citizens have also led to social change. People are choosing to have smaller families, for example. Spain is now an important member of the European Union (EU), which it joined in 1986. Like the United Kingdom, Spain has a constitutional monarch – King Juan Carlos. The king is the head of state, but the country is run by a government elected by the people.

Spain has achieved prominence in world sports, especially football, golf, tennis and cycling. The 1992 Olympic Games were hosted in Barcelona. Spain has a very rich and diverse cultural heritage (Madrid was the European City of Culture, also in 1992). Also, Spain's extensive, sun-drenched beaches, fine climate and varied landscapes make it one of the most popular tourist destinations in the world.

MODERN PROBLEMS

Despite Spain's assets, the country faces many problems. Along with other industrialised Western nations, it has environmental issues – water pollution, poor air quality in its cities, overuse of and dependency upon fossil fuels, global warming and its consequences – that need to be tackled by the government. Illegal immigration also continues to cause concern. Other social problems include high unemployment and a shortage of affordable housing for younger people.

Building boom – people play golf against a backdrop of new high-rise apartments.

Closely associated with the gypsies of Andalucía, flamenco is a highly stylised form of dance, song and guitar-playing that expresses the joys, sorrows and pain of life, especially concerning love. For a hundred years or more, it has been the music and expression of people on the margins of society. True flamenco is full of danger and excitement, but today some of this has been watered down to suit tourists. Andalucía is the flamenco heartland and its development has been influenced by the Jewish and Moorish communities of this region. Modern performers also improvise, adding their own interpretations of flamenco form, which means that it is constantly evolving.

Flamenco is usually performed in a bar or club. Typically there are four people on stage – a guitarist, singer, dancer and a hand-clapper, who helps keep the rhythm. There are different types of song (or *cante*) and dance. Rhythm is all-important and is emphasised by clapping, the clicking of

A flamenco hand-clapper, dancer and guitarist.

castanets, and the stamping and clicking heels of the male (*bailaor*) and female (*bailaora*) dancers. The audience often becomes involved, clapping, stamping and shouting *olés* as they encourage the dancer to greater demonstrations of what is called *duende*, the mysterious magic of flamenco.

Terrorism is also a major problem. On 11 March 2004, ten bombs exploded on four commuter trains on the outskirts of Madrid, killing 191 people and injuring almost 2,000. The attack was carried out by Moroccan extremists believed to have links with the terrorist group, Al Qaeda. The terrorists' aim was to influence the upcoming Spanish elections. The conservative government of José Maria Aznar (elected in 1996) supported the USA's involvement in Iraq, whereas the socialist opposition promised to withdraw Spanish troops from that country. The day after the bombings, twelve million Spanish people took to the streets to protest against the outrage. The government of José Maria Aznar was toppled in the elections and a new socialist government announced it was going to take Spanish troops out of Iraq.

Forensic experts examine trains damaged in the Madrid terrorist bombings of 11 March 2004.

LANDSCAPE AND CLIMATE

Sunbathers and swimmers enjoy the warm weather on a beach in Barcelona.

Spain has the most varied landscape of any country in Europe, ranging from hot beaches in the south to snow and glaciers in the high mountains. While the northern and western coastlines are green and wet, the vast interior of the country has parched deserts. The stunning volcanic scenery of the Canary Islands contrasts sharply with the wetlands and rivers of the mainland.

A CLIMATE OF EXTREMES

Spain's climate ranges from the hot, dry summers of the interior to the cold winter environment of the high mountains. While in winter the shores of Galicia in the north are windswept and rainy, the Mediterranean resorts of the south coast and the islands attract tourists in search of winter sun. In the centre of the country, the capital Madrid is many kilometres from any coast. Its continental climate means that temperatures are very hot in the summer (sometimes over 38°C) and cold in the winter (sometimes below freezing, with an average January temperature of 5°C). In comparison, the Canary Islands have a less extreme climate, with average daytime temperatures of 23°C or higher in the summer and 18°C in the winter.

CASE STUDY
THE MATORRAL

The region known as the Matorral, in the eastern Mediterranean corner of Spain, is well known for its great variety of wild flowers. In this region there has been widespread felling of indigenous trees, which means that the flowers have colonised the bare ground. The local climate – with moist springtimes, dry summers and mild winters – is perfect for these plants, and the scrubland soils suit the many aromatic herbs that flourish (such as sage, thyme, rosemary and lavender). Other species of plant growing in the Matorral include the yellow-flowering broom, orchids and several kinds of rock rose.

The nearness of the sea and its moderating influence means that the coasts remain temperate compared with the climate inland. On Spain's northern and westerly coasts, the huge Atlantic Ocean brings wet, cool weather. On Spain's southern coast, the relatively small, warm, enclosed Mediterranean Sea brings drier, warmer weather. The other factor that affects the climate is altitude. In the interior, the *Meseta* ranges from 600m to 1,000m in height and covers more than 200,000km^2. Its high altitude and distance from the sea produce extremes of temperature.

Spain has many high mountain ranges, some of which reach a maximum of almost 3,500m. Temperatures remain low in these mountains, and snow and ice lie on the ground all year round. Over the centuries the people living in the mountain villages have adapted to the particular conditions. They build houses with large, steep roofs for shedding snow, for example. In the spring, as the snows at lower altitudes begin to melt, the meadows are flecked with colourful alpine flowers.

Hikers climb Los Roques on Tenerife, Canary Islands, with Pico del Teide in the background.

CASE STUDY
THE CANARY ISLANDS

The Canaries are made up of seven main islands situated off the west coast of Morocco and are a major tourist destination. More than three million people visit Gran Canaria every year. Close to the Tropics, the Canaries are bathed in sunshine, but are also cooled by sea breezes. The Canaries consist of high volcanic peaks (the latest eruption was in the early 1970s), valley forests, lava deserts and wide sandy beaches. Tropical fruits such as bananas, mango, papaya and guava are all grown here.

LANDSCAPE FEATURES

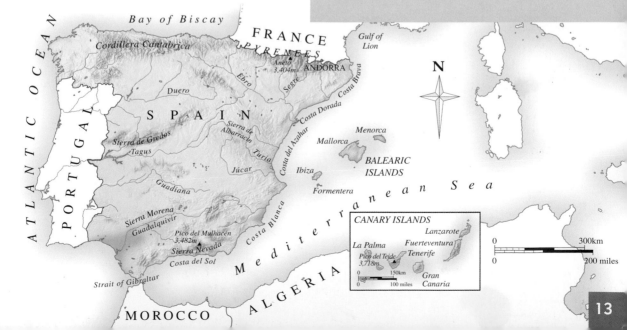

Bay of Biscay

ATLANTIC OCEAN

Cordillera Cantabrica

FRANCE

PYRENEES

Aneto 3,404m ANDORRA

Gulf of Lion

Duero

Ebro

Segre

Costa Brava

N

PORTUGAL

S P A I N

Sierra de Gredos

Tagus

Sierra de Albarracin

Turia

Júcar

Costa Dorada

Costa del Azahar

Costa Blanca

Menorca

Mallorca

Ibiza

Formentera

BALEARIC ISLANDS

Guadiana

Sierra Morena

Guadalquivir

Pico del Mulhacén 3,482m

Sierra Nevada

Costa del Sol

0   150km
0   100 miles

Strait of Gibraltar

M e d i t e r r a n e a n   S e a

CANARY ISLANDS

Lanzarote

La Palma

Fuerteventura

Tenerife

Pico del Teide 3,718m

0   150km
0   100 miles

Gran Canaria

ALGERIA

MOROCCO

0   300km
0   200 miles

LEFT: The ancient town of Córdoba, once capital of Moorish Spain, has grown up on the banks of the Guadalquivir River.

LANDSCAPE
RIVERS AND FLOODPLAINS

Given its size and the number of its mountain ranges, the Iberian Peninsula has surprisingly few large rivers. Consequently, water is a precious commodity in many parts of the country, especially in the dry interior where very little rain falls during the summer months.

Spain's major rivers include the Ebro, the Tagus, the Duero and the Guadalquivir. Of these, only the Ebro flows into the Mediterranean Sea; the others issue into the Atlantic Ocean. Many towns and cities have grown up on the banks of rivers, including Madrid, Córdoba, Sevilla, Cádiz, Tarragona, Valencia, Zaragoza, Barcelona and Bilbao. Rivers provide water for domestic use in the kitchen and household, as well as for agriculture and industry. Hydroelectric power (HEP) is an important source of energy in some parts of the country. Floodplains provide fertile land for growing crops. Here nutrient-rich river silt washes into the soil to give excellent growing conditions.

WETLANDS

Wetlands are made up of a mixture of landscapes – bogs and fens, reed beds, lakes, streams, freshwater marshes and coastal deltas. These are regions that flood occasionally and sometimes dry out completely, and they are important areas for wildlife.

The Coto de Doñana is a huge region (about 185,000 acres) formed from the delta of the mighty Guadalquivir River. It consists of marshes and sandy coastal stretches with dunes up to 30m high. It experiences drought in summer and flooding in winter. Migrating birds use it as a stopover on their journeys. Deer, wild cattle, wild boar, flamingos, eagles, and one of Europe's most endangered animals, the lynx, are found here. The area became the Doñana National Park in 1969.

The Tablas de Daimiel is another Spanish wetland. It was made a national park in 1973. It is a huge marsh region, north-east of Ciudad Real in Castilla-La Mancha. Situated a long way inland, it provides a much needed source of food and shelter for breeding and migratory birds.

The estuary of the Guadalquivir River, looking north towards the Doñana National Park.

A birdwatching observation tower in L'Albufera nature reserve.

L'Albufera is a large, shallow, freshwater lake in the east of Spain, and is one of the most important wetland habitats in this region. The Turia River drains into the lake, which is only about 2m deep. It is close to the sea, but separated from the salty water by a stretch of sandbank called the Dehesa. Reeds grow in the shallow waters and provide a perfect habitat for breeding birds, of which there are about 250 different species. L'Albufera became a nature reserve in 1986.

COASTAL REGIONS

Much of Spain's Atlantic coastline is rugged and eroded, and winter storms can be ferocious. The sea has carved parts of the coast into deep, fjord-like channels, called *rias*. Although it can be wild, the Atlantic is rich in fish. Major ports along this coast include La Coruña, Santander, Bilbao and Vigo. East of La Coruña, the Costa Verde extends through the regions of Asturias and Cantabria. Here the coastline is less rugged, and holidaymakers flock to its sandy beaches and coves.

The Mediterranean is a large inland sea between southern Europe, North Africa and south-west Asia. Over thousands of years of human settlement, fishing ports have grown up along Spain's sheltered Mediterranean coast. They include Algeciras, Málaga, Valencia and Barcelona. This coast has seen huge development since the late 1950s. Hotels, bars and restaurants catering for the tourist trade have transformed sleepy fishing villages into vast urban sprawls – especially along the Costa del Sol (from the border of Cádiz province to Almería) and the Costa Blanca (around Alicante and Benidorm).

The hostile and barren landscape of the Tabernas Desert in southern Spain.

DESERTS AND ARID LAND

In Andalucía, in the region north of the coastal town of Almeria, is the Tabernas Desert, a landscape unique in all Europe. This is Europe's only true mainland desert. Almeria is situated at the eastern end of the Sierra Nevada mountain range and in its rain shadow. This rain shadow is largely responsible for creating the desert conditions here. Most of the rain in the region arrives on westerly winds and falls mainly on the high ground of the Sierra Nevada. Often there is no rainfall in the desert from April to November.

A DRY INTERIOR

Apart from this desert, much of the rest of the interior of the country is semi-desert or arid (dry) land where little rain falls. The regions most affected are Extremadura, Castilla-La Mancha and Castilla y León. Arid landscapes are on the increase in Spain, making it difficult to keep the soil fertile enough to grow crops.

Certain types of farming practice have made the problem worse. For example, farmers have felled trees to clear the land for growing crops. By doing so, they have opened up their fields to wind erosion. Trees provide some shelter and take the force of autumn winds.

Cork oak forests (and goats) are a common sight in parts of Spain. They thrive in the dry interior.

Once they are removed, soil is easily blown away. Large cities in these dry plains (including Madrid, Salamanca, Toledo and Valladolid) use an enormous amount of water for domestic and industrial use, and they take this water from the surrounding land.

WOODS AND WOODLAND

Just 10 per cent of the forest that originally covered Spain remains today. Nevertheless Spain has a surprising variety of woodlands, from the farmed cork oak plantations in Extremadura on the border with Portugal, to the great beech, oak and chestnut woods of Galicia, Cantabria and the Basque Country. In Andalucía there are olive groves, while pine forests cloak the slopes of the Pyrenees. La Gomera, one of the smaller of the Canary Islands, has a forested national park region, the Parque Nacional de Garajonay.

A view of Pico del Mulhacén, covered in snow. This is the highest point of the Sierra Nevada mountain range, seen from the Alhambra, above the city of Granada.

THE MOUNTAINS OF SPAIN

Spain has many mountain ranges, including the Sierra Nevada in the south, and the Cordillera Cantabrica and the Pyrenees Mountains in the north. The Pyrenees extend in a chain for 440km from the Bay of Biscay in the west to the Mediterranean Sea in the east. They form a continuous border with France and are a considerable barrier, complete with snow, ice, and even small glaciers. The highest Pyrenean peak is Aneto (3,404m). Pico del Mulhacén (3,482m) in the Sierra Nevada is the highest mountain on the Spanish mainland. The Sierra Nevada also has one of the highest roads in Europe. Overall, Spain's tallest mountain is Pico del Teide (3,718m) in the Canaries. In addition to the principal mountain ranges, there are numerous other smaller and less well-known regions, such as the Sierra de Gredos to the west of Madrid, which reaches 2,500m, and the Sierra de Alberracin, north-west of Valencia.

Torrential rain pours off a roof in Córdoba.

CLIMATE AND WEATHER

Spain's great diversity of landscape and climate means that there is a huge variety of vegetation growing throughout the country. Desert cacti, Barbary figs, chestnut and oak forests, and meadow flowers all thrive in the rich natural environment.

Influenced by the Atlantic Ocean, the north and west coasts have a temperate maritime climate. Although the sea takes longer to heat up than the land, it stays warm for longer. This means it continues to warm the coastal regions long after the land itself has cooled down in the autumn and winter. This is the region of the Costa Verde, the green coast. Rainfall is plentiful throughout the year, especially during winter.

INTERIOR REGIONS

In Spain's interior regions, the winters are freezing (with temperatures as low as –10°C in January, compared with an average temperature of 5°C on the south coast and a balmy 18°C in the Canary Islands during the same month). The summers are hot and dry, with temperatures frequently exceeding 38°C. These extremes of temperature are typical of what is called a continental climate. One factor in this is distance from the sea, which gives rise to a climate of greater extremes and drier conditions.

MEDITERRANEAN REGIONS

Many people like to retire to the Mediterranean coast because of its hot, dry summers and mild winters. The absence of extreme weather patterns is typical of this climate. Many different kinds of fruits and vegetables grow well here. Citrus fruits,

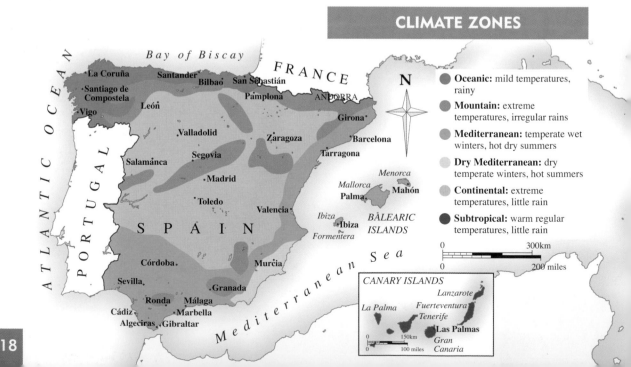

CLIMATE ZONES

- **Oceanic:** mild temperatures, rainy
- **Mountain:** extreme temperatures, irregular rains
- **Mediterranean:** temperate wet winters, hot dry summers
- **Dry Mediterranean:** dry temperate winters, hot summers
- **Continental:** extreme temperatures, little rain
- **Subtropical:** warm regular temperatures, little rain

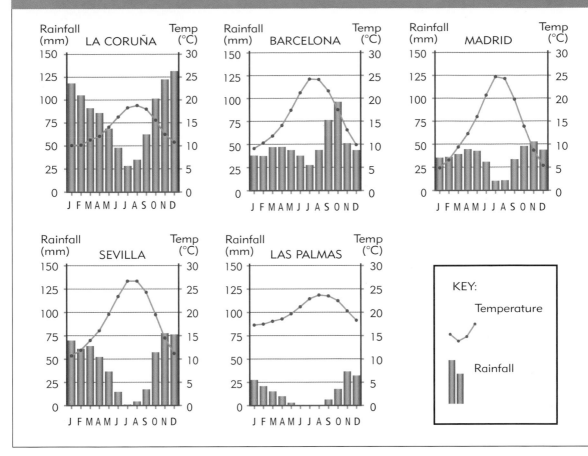

LA CORUÑA — Rainfall (mm) / Temp (°C)

BARCELONA — Rainfall (mm) / Temp (°C)

MADRID — Rainfall (mm) / Temp (°C)

SEVILLA — Rainfall (mm) / Temp (°C)

LAS PALMAS — Rainfall (mm) / Temp (°C)

KEY:

Temperature

Rainfall

apricots, tomatoes, salad greens, olives, grapes and grains all flourish in a landscape that receives plenty of sunshine and seasonal rain brought in on westerly winds during the autumn and winter months.

MOUNTAINOUS REGIONS

The mountainous regions of the country have higher precipitation (more rain and snow), colder winter temperatures and are cooler on average in the summer than the surrounding lowlands. Skiing takes place in the Sierra Nevada and the Pyrenees during the winter months. The vegetation is typical of that adapted to high pastures and mountains – pine trees that can withstand cold temperatures and brightly coloured alpine meadow flowers, such as gentian, which add splendour to the scenery in June and July. Animals such as the chamois (a type of antelope found across the mountain ranges

A palm tree grows in the sunshine of south-west Spain.

of Europe) and marmots (large rodents) live on the high, remote slopes of the mountains, and are perfectly adapted to the harsh and bleak conditions.

PEOPLE OF SPAIN

Like most nations in Europe, the Spanish are a mixture of races, with a great variety of skin colour and features.

Over a period of 700 years, settlers from the Islamic kingdoms on the other side of the Mediterranean intermingled with the peoples of southern Spain. The result of this mix means that many Spanish people have dark skin, hair and eyes. However, some Spanish people are fair-haired (even red-headed) and have light-coloured eyes. This is because peoples such as the Celts, Romans and even the Visigoths (a Germanic people who invaded Spain for a brief period in the sixth century) also left a genetic legacy.

POPULATION

Spain today has a population growth that is in reverse. It is estimated that, at the current rate of decline, the population will start to fall dramatically in the next ten years. The reasons for this are socially complex. However, increased wealth and the growth of the middle classes has led to a significant shift in the priorities of family life. Today, instead of having large families, younger people are choosing to pursue better paid jobs and a higher standard of living.

RELIGION

About 94 per cent of Spaniards are Roman Catholics, and the family and Church still

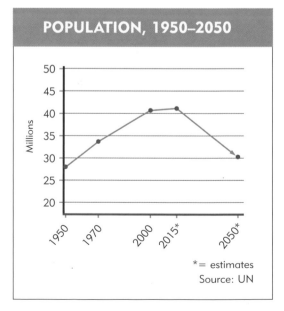

POPULATION, 1950–2050

*= estimates
Source: UN

RIGHT: Crowds gather at a festival in the village of El Rocio, southern Spain, to worship the statue of the Madonna of the Dew.

figure strongly in the lives of many citizens. A large number of public holidays are based around religious festivals – not just Christmas and Easter, but Epiphany (6 January), Assumption (15 August), All Saints' Day (1 November), and Immaculate Conception Day (8 December). Other minority religions include Islam and Judaism. Historically, Christians, Muslims and Jews have lived together peacefully for long periods, interspersed with short bursts of intolerance and persecution. The Jews came to Spain at the time of the ancient Greeks. They became particularly influential in the southern cities of Toledo, Córdoba and Sevilla. These cities still retain links with their Jewish past – Córdoba, for example, has an area of the city called the *Juderia*.

MINORITY GROUPS

Spain is home to many minority communities, including gypsies and people from North Africa. Tensions exist between the majority of Spaniards and these minority groups. Gypsies are often seen as outsiders because of their different customs and lifestyles. North Africans form a large immigrant population, many of

whom have a legal right to be in the country. However, many do not, and desperate people looking for a better life and the chance to earn a living arrive regularly from Morocco. Unscrupulous farmers and businessmen use them as cheap labour. The immigrants often send money home to their families while working illegally in Spain. Those caught by the police are sent back to Morocco.

CASE STUDY
BULLFIGHTING

Bullfighting originated in the town of Ronda in the seventeenth century and is as popular in Spain today as it ever was. There are bullrings in many towns and cities and fights attract large crowds, especially at festival time. Bullfights are very ritualised: each stage and movement has a special name, as do the different people who take part in them. For example, *picadores* on horseback ride

around the bull to goad it to anger; *banderillos* then stick darts into the animal's back and neck; and finally the *matador* appears with his cloak to pit himself against the beast. Famous matadors of the past can often be seen in old photographs and paintings in bars and restaurants from Madrid to Barcelona. Some people see bullfighting as a cruel and unnecessary form of entertainment. But most Spanish people do not want to see it stopped or banned. They see it as an important aspect of Spanish culture and tradition.

CULTURE AND TRADITION

Spain's rich cultural history is evident throughout the country. There are museums with artefacts such as Celtic bowls made from beaten gold over 2,000 years old, Greek vases from the sixth century BC, Roman coins, and Christian crosses from the age of the Visigoths. There are ancient structures, such as the famous Roman aqueduct at Segovia, north-west of Madrid, or the imposing amphitheatre at Tarragona on the coast south-west of Barcelona. In the south, especially in Andalucía, Islamic and Christian traditions combine in the great monuments of the past, such as the Alhambra in Granada and the Great Mosque in Córdoba. The country is also littered with thousands of castles, testament to a time of local warfare and feudal strife, from the Moorish occupation to the sixteenth century.

Spanish people have a passion for classical opera and Spain has produced world-class singers, such as Placido Domingo and José Carreras. There is also a wealth of works of art, from medieval and Renaissance religious art to the great late nineteenth- and twentieth-century artists such as Juan Grís, Salvador Dali and Pablo Picasso. Spain's culture is also evident in its literature. *Don Quixote* by Miguel

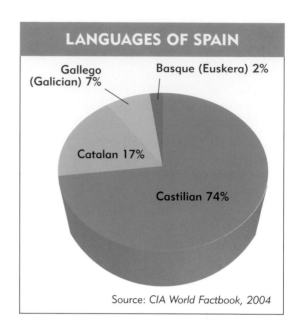

LANGUAGES OF SPAIN

Gallego (Galician) 7%

Basque (Euskera) 2%

Catalan 17%

Castilian 74%

Source: *CIA World Factbook, 2004*

Cervantes (1547–1616) was one of the first novels ever written. Modern writers include Juan Marse and Eduardo Mendoza and the playwright, Antonio Gala. In the film-making industry, Pedro Almodovar stands out as a world-class director, with films such as *Women on the Edge of a Nervous Breakdown*.

FOOD AND DRINK

The Spanish are proud of their cuisine. Fine fruit, vegetables, fish and meat products find their way into a bewildering number of regional dishes and are accompanied by wine, cider and other drinks such as sherry (see page 36), a drink from the Cádiz area. In the north, seafood from the Atlantic is a popular ingredient of numerous fish dishes, including *txangurro relleno* made from spider crab. Octopus, scallops, mussels and prawns are also popular ingredients. Cattle are raised in the green pastures of the north to produce cheese and other dairy products. *Tetilla, cabrales* and *idiazabal* are all local cheeses from the north. A regional meat and vegetable stew is called *el caldo gallego*.

In Cataluña, the ingredients and influences are different. Here olives, citrus fruits, rice and nuts add flavour to dishes of prawns, eggs, black sausage and chicken. This is a Mediterranean cuisine, but it is heavily

Built in 1997, the Guggenheim in Bilbao is one of the world's leading art museums.

People eating *tapas* (see page 49) in a bar in San Sebastian, northern Spain.

influenced by North African recipes and ingredients introduced to Spain many centuries ago. People keep pigs in the hills and mountains of Cataluña, and make different varieties of sausage including the *butifarra*, or white sausage, the *fuet* and the *llangonisseta*.

Further south, in Andalucía, grilled fish and deep-fried *calamares* (squid) appear on the menu. *Jamon serrano*, a type of cured ham, can be found hanging in shops in every town in the south. The best comes from the town of Trevélez in the Alpujarra. Another favourite dish of the region is *gazpacho*, a chilled soup made with cucumbers, tomatoes, peppers and garlic. Delicate biscuits made with almonds and cinnamon are also a speciality.

A shop selling cheeses and chorizo sausage in the town of Aranjuez.

As a result of their geographical position and history, the cuisine of the Canary Islands exhibits influences from Africa and South America. Sweetcorn (maize) and bananas are eaten widely, and rum has been made on the islands for hundreds of years, reflecting a link with the Caribbean.

POPULATION STRUCTURE, 2004

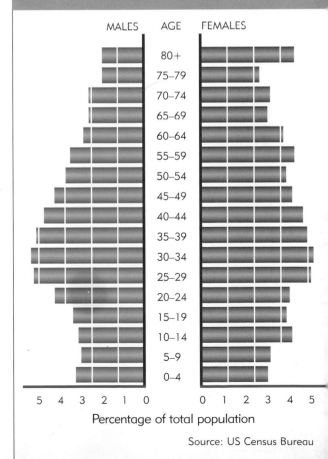

Percentage of total population

Source: US Census Bureau

THE POLITICS OF REGIONALISM

Geographical regions are important to the Spanish identity. Politically, Spain is less centralised than other countries in the European Union. The 1978 constitution, drawn up at the wishes of the new king, Juan Carlos, transferred some powers to regional capitals. While Madrid remained the centre of national government, 17 regional governments, known as *communidadas autonomas* were created. Central government controls defence, foreign policy and general taxation. Local governments have power over education, health and social services, although central government sets their budgets. The local governments of the Basque Country in the north and Cataluña in the north-east have more political power than any other administrative region outside Madrid.

THE REGIONS OF SPAIN

An ETA demonstration in Bilbao, capital of the Basque Country. People hold the Basque flag, known as the 'ikurrina'.

The Spanish are generally very proud of their regions: wherever you go, people will claim that the local food, football teams, and even the languages are the best in Spain. Mostly, this fierce regional loyalty is a positive force in Spanish life. However, there is a darker aspect to it. A few of the regions (Galicia, Cataluña and the Basque Country) have looked for complete independence from the rest of Spain. Some people have turned to violence to achieve their political goals.

INDEPENDENCE AND TERRORISM

In the Basque Country, the desire for independence led in 1959 to the formation of ETA, the Basque separatist organisation. ETA works in a similar way to the Irish Republican Army (IRA) in Ireland. Its members have used terrorist tactics to try to get what they want – setting off bombs and assassinating politicians and prominent public figures. The Spanish government has worked hard to try to capture militant ETA members. Despite the government's efforts, ETA is still active today.

CATALUÑA

Cataluña has been described as a nation within a nation. It has a culture, history and language so different from the rest of Spain that some people feel it should be totally independent. The area includes the cities of Barcelona (the region's capital), Lleida, Tarragona and Girona. It is bounded to the north and east by the Pyrenees and to the south by the Mediterranean Sea. The Costa Brava, one of the most heavily developed tourist regions in Spain, is also part of Cataluña. Under General Franco, all books and newspapers written in Catalan were destroyed and the language was banned. Since Franco's death there has been a flourishing of the Catalan tongue, along with literature and arts in general. Today, street and road signs are written in Catalan, not Castilian. People speak habitually in their language, which is taught in schools.

A procession through streets carpeted with flowers during the *Festa de Corpus Christi* in Sitges.

CASE STUDY
THE FIESTA OF CATALUÑA

Catalans enjoy celebrating and they have a number of *fiesta* (festivals) unique to their region. In every month of the year there is a major festival taking place somewhere in Cataluña. The *Pelegri de Tossa* is a pilgrimage from the seaside town of Tossa to Santa Colomba to honour Saint Sebastian. It takes place on 20 January, and is followed by the festivities of a winter fair. There is a carnival at Sitges, a fishing port about 40km from Barcelona. This takes place over a number of days in late February and early March. It consists of masked balls and parades through the streets and is very theatrical and colourful. Eating, drinking, listening to bands and joining in with the processions are all very much part of the fun. Sitges also hosts a *fiesta* in May, called the *Festa de Corpus Christi*. On 24 June, all over the region, shops and businesses close for a day or two for the *Dia de Sant Joan*. This *fiesta* involves fireworks, processions and bonfires (*fallas*).

RESOURCES, INDUSTRY AND TRANSPORT

The Vandellos Dos nuclear power plant in Tarragona. Spain currently has nine nuclear power stations.

Under General Franco, Spain was cut off from the industrial and economic development that was occurring in France, the UK and Germany during much of the twentieth century. By the United Nations' definition, Spain was an agrarian developing country in a position similar to that of many Eastern European countries today. It had some industry, but very little compared with the majority of its richer neighbours. The state of communications was poor. Spain's underdeveloped road and railway networks hampered the growth of trade and industry.

THE STABILISATION PLAN

In the 1960s, still under Franco's repressive regime, Spain began to change. The 1950s had seen the nation slide into poverty and high inflation. By 1959, the situation was so bad that the government brought in strong measures to reverse the trend. This was called the Stabilisation Plan. Its aim was to modernise the country and raise the living standards and income of the people. Between 1960 and 1970, car ownership increased from about one person in one hundred to one in ten of the population. The country began to invest heavily in its industrial development.

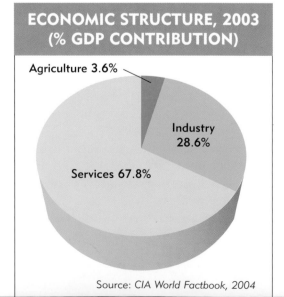

ECONOMIC STRUCTURE, 2003 (% GDP CONTRIBUTION)

Agriculture 3.6%

Industry 28.6%

Services 67.8%

Source: *CIA World Factbook, 2004*

The city of Bilbao has one of the largest steelworks in Europe. It is one of Spain's most important, productive industrial centres, and is a main port for the import and export of goods. Iron and steel production have been important in the region since the late nineteenth century. It was one of the very few areas of Spain to undergo anything close to the Industrial Revolution that was experienced by other Western European countries at this time.

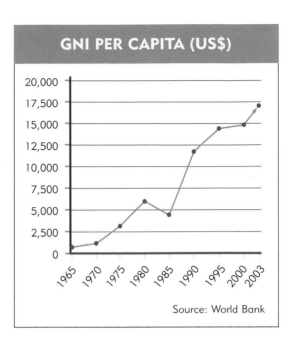

GNI PER CAPITA (US$)

Source: World Bank

A greater number of raw materials were extracted, steel plants, chemical factories, car manufacturing plants and shipyards were built, and cities grew in size and population.

Between 1961 and 1974, the average increase in the nation's wealth was 7 per cent, far higher than any other country, apart from Japan, at that time. Spain had deliberately set its sights on catching up with other Western economies. Even in agriculture, Spain started to become mechanised. For example, by the 1970s there were far more tractors on the land. Spain became the world's biggest producer and exporter of olive oil.

Franco's death led to a further acceleration of progress as the country started a process of liberalisation. Today, Spain has the fifth largest economy in Europe and is a major producer and exporter of industrial goods.

THE EUROPEAN UNION

By the 1980s, Spain's economy had leapt ahead, assisted by its entry into the European Union in 1986. It now had one of the fastest growing economies anywhere in the world and was among the first countries to adopt the Euro, the new European currency launched on 1 January 1999. Spain's economic growth has been the result of developing industry and services. Tourism, for example, adds around £30 billion to the economy every year (8 per cent of the national income, and twice that of all agricultural income).

MAJOR TRADING PARTNERS (% OF VALUE), 2003

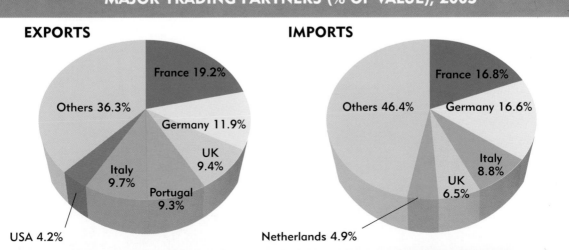

EXPORTS

France 19.2%
Germany 11.9%
UK 9.4%
Portugal 9.3%
Italy 9.7%
Others 36.3%
USA 4.2%

IMPORTS

France 16.8%
Germany 16.6%
Italy 8.8%
UK 6.5%
Others 46.4%
Netherlands 4.9%

Source: CIA World Factbook, 2004

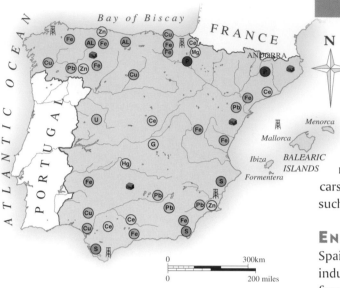

Petroleum		Cement	
Coal		Aluminium	
Iron and steel		Mercury	
Zinc		Uranium	
Copper		Potash	
Lead		Salt	
Magnesium		Gypsum	

Spain exports metals and products made from metal, such as machinery and cars, to the rest of Europe, and imports items such as fuel, chemicals and consumer goods.

ENERGY

Spain derives most of its energy for powering industry and lighting and heating homes from fossil fuels – by burning coal, oil and gas. Coal-fired power stations, which convert the energy into electricity, meet more than half the country's needs. Other sources of energy include HEP (hydroelectric power) stations, which change the power of moving water into electricity. HEP accounts for over 18 per cent of the total electricity supply.

NUCLEAR POWER

Nuclear power stations generate more than 27 per cent of all Spain's electricity. Spain currently has nine nuclear power stations. The first (the José Cabrera) was built in 1968 and others followed in the 1970s and 1980s.

NATURAL RESOURCES

In terms of raw materials, Spain has reserves of coal, oil and gas. It has metals, including iron, lead, zinc, copper, mercury, tungsten and uranium. These are mined and used in various industrial processes, including the nuclear industry. Metal production is one of Spain's main heavy industries, along with shipbuilding. Gypsum is a soft mineral found in Spain. It has many uses, for example in the making of casts, moulds and blackboard chalk.

A large open-cast copper mine in Rio Tinto, Andalucía.

ELECTRICITY PRODUCTION BY SOURCE, 2001

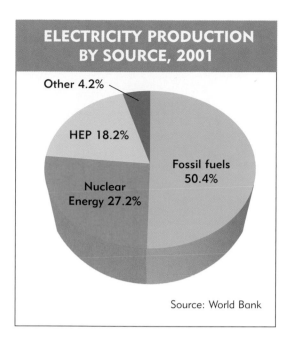

- Other 4.2%
- HEP 18.2%
- Fossil fuels 50.4%
- Nuclear Energy 27.2%

Source: World Bank

A small HEP station in southern Spain.

In common with all advanced Western industrial nations, Spain depends upon its nuclear power to support fossil fuel and renewable sources of energy. Without nuclear power, the Spanish would have to burn far more coal and oil. While many people do not like nuclear power, it has become accepted by the general population, despite the fact that environmentalists constantly campaign to have it replaced. Although nuclear fuel is relatively clean and does not produce greenhouse gases, environmentalists argue that it is difficult and dangerous to dispose of the spent uranium rods from old nuclear power stations. Like the rest of the world, the Spanish have not found an answer to this problem.

RENEWABLE ENERGY

Spain has few rivers for such a big country, but the ones it has are large and provide plenty of power. HEP stations can be found at Porma and Puron, both in the Cordillera Cantabrica mountain range in the north, Suso on the River Cardenas in Rioja, El Chorro, not far from Málaga on the south coast, in Castilla y León in central Spain, and on the Guadalquivir River at Hurones in Andalucía. Between them, these HEP stations generate almost one fifth of the nation's electricity.

Plants that harness the power of the wind can be found at Tarazona Sur, at Tarifa on the coast facing Morocco, and on the island of Menorca. They are also springing up on Spain's northern coast, in Galicia and Asturias, where wind is a feature of the weather. Wind farms make only a small contribution to the national grid supply, but they may well be pointing the way to the future of renewable energy sources. Wind farm development is a growth area. It is popular with the government and with many environmentalists. But a significant number of people are against its expansion, for several reasons. Wind farms take up a great deal of space and are considered unsightly. They cost a lot of money to install and are not very efficient. And, of course, when the wind does not blow, they do not work.

In common with other nations, Spain's demand for energy is likely to increase in the future. At the moment, over half the needs are met by using fossil fuels such as coal, oil and gas. This situation is likely to change. There is concern over just how long the supplies of fossils fuels will last. There is also concern over the fact that significant quantities of oil come from the Middle East, a politically unstable part of the world.

A wind farm near Tarifa on the southern coast.

MANUFACTURING AND CONSTRUCTION

Today Spain's wealth is based upon a mixed capitalist economy, consisting of companies and industries that produce all sorts of goods and services for sale at home and abroad. These range from huge multi-million dollar companies involved in shipbuilding, car manufacturing, chemical production and mining, to smaller companies involved in other important activities, such as textile and footwear manufacture and food and drink production. The tourist industry supports many different businesses, such as hotels, catering and holiday companies, suppliers (of food and drink, for example), car hire companies, airlines, and so on.

CASE STUDY
SEAT

The Spanish-based car manufacturing company, Seat, was set up in 1950. Different types of Seat cars are given atmospheric Spanish names like 'Ibiza', 'Leon', 'Cordoba', 'Toledo' and 'Alhambra'. Seat is owned, however, by the German car-manufacturing giant, Audi-Volkswagen, which means that Seat engineers and designers have access to some of the most advanced car technology in the world.

The car plant is based at Martorell. In 2003, it manufactured 436,933 units and had a turnover of €5,523,000,000. The plant is one of the newest in Europe and was opened in 1993 by King Juan Carlos. It currently has 1,250 engineers working on existing and new ranges of car. Worldwide, Seat employs more than 13,000 people, most of them in Spain itself. About one third of all Seat cars produced in Spain are sold in Spain. The other two thirds are exported, mostly to neighbouring European countries such as France, the UK and Germany.

Assembly-line workers at the Seat factory in Martorell.

TOLEDO STEEL

It is thought that the Romans started the tradition of sword-making in the region of Toledo, a city about 70km south-west of Madrid. The quality of the Toledo steel used in sword-making has become world famous. It is often highly decorated, the black steel inlaid with copper, gold and steel filigree.

A manager stands outside a new asphalt plant on the outskirts of Baena, Andalucía. Asphalt is used in road construction.

Road-building and construction play a major role in the economy of the country. There are huge schemes taking place to develop and improve the infrastructure and communication networks. Materials, such as asphalt for road construction and cement for building houses, are supplied by an increasing number of production plants. Construction companies employ labour and need new machinery to move building materials and prepare the ground for construction to take place.

A builder's yard on the edge of a small town in southern Spain.

TRANSPORT NETWORKS

Spain's industry is aided by its fast and efficient road, rail and air transport systems. Since the mid-1980s, successive governments have developed and expanded all forms of transport communications. Along with many other things, modern transport has come late to Spain. In the past this delay hampered trade and industry because it was not easy to move goods or people around. All this has changed, however. A great deal of European Union money has been used to help Spain improve

Abando metro station in Bilbao. The Bilbao metro was opened in 2002.

its standards of road and rail transport along the lines of countries such as Germany and France. Spain has ambitious plans to continue this development well into the future. In the main cities of Madrid, Barcelona, Bilbao and Valencia, underground networks are already in place and Sevilla is currently constructing its own metro system.

TRANSPORT

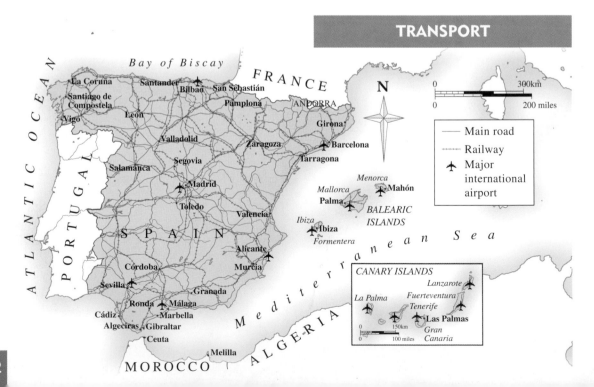

GROWTH OF THE NETWORKS

Since the mid-1980s, there has been a five-fold increase in motorway construction in Spain. There were 2,000km of motorway in the 1980s; today there are almost 11,000km. There are plans to build more than 10,000km of new roads by 2007 and to widen and modernise existing roads. Madrid is the centre of the communications network. Across the country, faster roads linking towns and villages are being constructed all the time.

There are also measures underway to extend the high-speed rail links between main cities. The Spanish government wants to increase these by 1,200km. The Andalucían rail express is a good example of modern rail links. It connects Madrid with Córdoba, Sevilla and Cádiz, and transports business people and holidaymakers quickly and efficiently to the south. A high-speed rail link has been completed between Madrid and Lleida in eastern Spain. By 2007, this will reach Barcelona. The Spanish are working with the French to construct a rail tunnel through the Pyrenees, linking Barcelona with Perpignan in France. This will give Spain access to the French high-speed rail network, the TGV, and will connect the country directly with the rest of Europe.

Other plans include fast rail links between Madrid and Valladolid to the north-west (already under construction), to Valencia on the south coast, to Lisbon, the capital of Portugal, to the west, and between Córdoba and Málaga in the south. Perhaps Spain's most ambitious goal is to build a tunnel beneath the Strait of Gibraltar that will link mainland Spain with North Africa.

There are 156 airports in Spain. Of these, 95 have paved runways to facilitate the landing of larger passenger airplanes. There are 30 airports handling international flights. All main cities (such as Madrid, Barcelona, Bilbao, Valencia, Cádiz and Sevilla) have their own airports. There are smaller destinations that are important for the tourist industry – including Alicante, Lanzarote, Santiago de Compostela and Las Palmas. The state-owned airline is Iberia Airlines. It runs international flights around the world as well as internal ones between Spanish cities.

SPAIN'S TRANSPORT SYSTEMS (TOTAL LENGTH)

Railways	14,189km
Roads	663,795km (including 10,317km of motorways)
Waterways	1,045km (of minor economic importance)
Pipelines	gas 7,290km
	oil 730km

The fast, modern Andalucían express train makes its way across the *Meseta* on route from Madrid to Cádiz.

Modern farming practices in Spain have featured a marked increase in the ownership of tractors.

I n the early twentieth century, most people in Spain worked on the land or in the fishing industry. Over 50 per cent of the country's exports were agricultural. Grain production alone was five times more profitable than coal, iron and steel production. Although agriculture is still important, today it accounts for only 3.6 per cent of the country's income, compared with 28.6 per cent generated by industry.

FARMING

One hundred years ago, most people worked on small farms producing food for themselves and the local population, or on large scale estates owned by rich aristocrats. Today, barely 7 per cent of the working population earns a living from farming, compared with 64 per cent working in services, mostly in towns and cities, and almost 30 per cent in construction, manufacturing and mining. Those still employed in farming work on much larger holdings that are more efficient and profitable than they used to be. A lot of produce is grown for the export market: Spanish melons, aubergines, tomatoes, courgettes, lettuces, strawberries and peppers, for example, are regularly seen on supermarket shelves in Germany and the UK.

In many areas, farmers use modern techniques, including growing fruit, vegetables and flowers under plastic which provides protection from inclement weather and maximises the effects of the sun. Huge areas of the Spanish countryside are now covered in plastic, and produce can be grown all year round.

TYPES OF PRODUCE

The diversity of Spain's geography and climate means that a wide range of fruits and vegetables can be grown. For example, olives, grapes, figs and citrus fruits are grown on the sunny, frost free Mediterranean coast and hinterland. Spain is the world's biggest producer of olive oil, much of which is from the province of Jaén in Andalucía. There are

PRINCIPAL CROPS

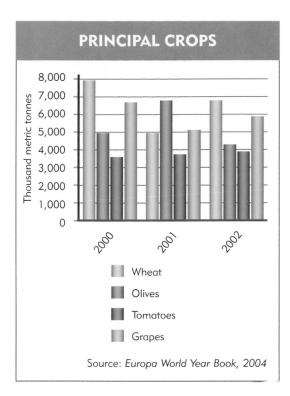

Thousand metric tonnes (y-axis, values 0 to 8,000)
Years: 2000, 2001, 2002

- Wheat
- Olives
- Tomatoes
- Grapes

Source: *Europa World Year Book, 2004*

Locally produced cheeses from Galicia, a region renowned for its dairy produce.

also plenty of market garden products from these areas, including salad vegetables such as tomatoes, aubergines and peppers.

In the dry interior, much of the land is given over to grain production. Cereals, such as wheat and barley, are important crops. Rice is grown in the wetter eastern regions where seasonal flooding takes place, for example, on the delta of the Ebro River near Valencia. The rice is harvested in September. On the *Meseta*

sheep are reared for their meat and wool, and their milk is used to make cheese. *Manchego* is a very well known sheep's cheese from the region of Castilla-La Mancha. If allowed to mature it hardens, and is highly prized for its flavour and texture.

In the wetter, milder conditions of northern Spain, dairy cattle thrive. Galicia is well known for its large number of cheeses, especially the soft variety, such as *tetilla*. Pigs are also farmed and their meat is used to make sausages, among other things. There are many different regional varieties of these sausages, of which the Spanish are very fond.

An olive tree plantation in the countryside near the city of Córdoba.

A worker checks the quality of grapes growing at a vineyard in north-west Spain.

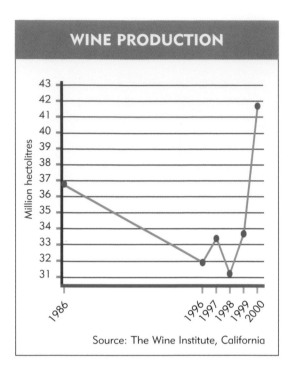

WINE PRODUCTION

Graph showing Million hectolitres for years 1986, 1996, 1997, 1998, 1999, 2000.

Source: The Wine Institute, California

WINE PRODUCTION

Spain is one of the world's main wine producers, generating more than 41 million hectolitres in 2000 (one hectolitre = 100 litres). More land is given over to growing grapes in Spain than in any other country. Wine is an important export and a staple drink of the Spanish people. One of the best known wine-producing regions is Rioja, situated in north-eastern Spain. Many varieties of white wine are produced in Galicia and the Basque Country, while sparkling wine is produced in Cataluña.

Several thousand years ago, the ancient Greeks planted and tended vines along the coast of southern Spain. The tradition has continued to this day, as grapes grow well in places that receive lots of sunlight, some rain, and little or no frost.

On average, Spain produces about 35 million hectolitres of wine every year. The export market in wine is worth in the region of US$1.2 billion per year. This is a considerable contribution to the Spanish economy. However, Spain has suffered some serious droughts in the recent past. These have adversely affected the grape yield and wine production. Although some 3.5 million acres of land are devoted to growing grapes for the wine industry, the dry and harsh conditions of the Spanish interior mean that Spain produces less wine than countries such as France and the USA, both of which have less land under vine cultivation.

SHERRY

The most well-known sherry-producing region is Jerez (which is where the word sherry comes from), near the port of Cádiz. Sherry is a wine that has been fortified, or made stronger in alcohol content. The sherry export market is very important to the economy of these southern rural regions. On average, about 666,600 hectolitres of sherry are produced every year.

FISHING

The Spanish consume more fish and seafood than any other nation in Europe. Their fishing fleets have been important to the local and national economy for hundreds of years and Spain still has one of the largest fleets in the world. Most of what they catch is for the home market, though some fresh produce is exported. Today Spain imports large quantities of fish from other countries because her fleets cannot keep up with the demand.

Over half of all fish and seafood caught in Spain comes from Galicia. Almost 100,000 Galicians are employed in fishing, and they land over a million tonnes every year, including tuna, sardines, lobster, crabs and clams. Spain's northern coastline is studded with little fishing ports such as Castropol and Figueras. Seafood restaurants are numerous along the coast and into the Basque Country. Special regional dishes include *empanada* (a pie with salt cod and seafood) and *revuelto*

Unloading tuna from a freezer ship at the fishing port of Ribeira in Galicia.

(eggs and prawns). In the south, the Mediterranean Sea has been extensively over-fished and its yields are small compared with what they once were. However, measures to protect fish and seafood stocks have helped with some species.

Fishing boats at a small port in Galicia.

CASE STUDY
VIGO: SPAIN'S MAJOR FISHING PORT

Vigo, in the far north-west of Spain, is the biggest fishing port in the country. It is situated on a deep channel called the Ria de Vigo. There are treacherous sandbanks in parts of the Ria. In 1702, a fleet of ships carrying an enormous quantity of silver was sunk there while sheltering from a storm. Today, a large suspension bridge spans the Ria de Vigo. The harbour where fishing vessels shelter is enclosed and well protected from the Atlantic storms, and the quayside along which the boats moor is 5km long. There is a large fishmarket, and there are dozens of *tapas* bars (see pages 23 and 49) selling drinks and seafood snacks.

In the *Mezquita* (mosque) at Córdoba, tourists photograph the *Mihrab*, a beautifully decorated niche that points the faithful towards Mecca.

S pain has been a popular European tourist destination since the late 1950s when the first chartered holiday flights were introduced, and it has been associated with mass-market package holidays ever since. Today about 60 million tourists visit Spain each year, and there are around one million hotels and other types of accommodation to cater for them.

Most of Spain's tourists visit from other European countries such as France, Germany, Holland, Belgium, the UK, Sweden and Norway. The tourist industry accounts for around 8 per cent of the country's income, and about fifteen out of every hundred working people in Spain are employed in tourism. The Spanish economy is therefore very vulnerable to fluctuations in tourist numbers and to changing tastes in holiday destinations.

HOT SPOTS

The most popular month on the tourist calendar is August, when about ten million tourists arrive in Spain. This means that, on average, every fifth person in the country is a tourist. The most popular destination is the

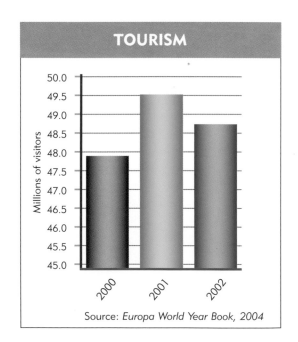

Source: *Europa World Year Book, 2004*

There are four main Balearic Islands – Mallorca, Menorca, Ibiza and Formentera. Tourism has left its mark on all of them, with roads, hotels, ports, airports, golf courses and swimming pools. While the coasts are given over to tourism, evidence of past agricultural ways of life still exists inland. Mallorca has a rugged interior that is a popular destination with cyclists who come to test their skill against the hilly roads. Rock climbers also seek out the secluded cliffs of the coast and the gorges of the interior.

island of Mallorca (see case study), which attracts around three million people every year. The proximity of the sea, the sunny climate and the relatively low cost of living have fuelled the island's economy since it became a package-holiday destination in the 1960s and 1970s. In recent years, however, the authorities have made attempts to attract the more up-market tourist. Today, film stars (such as Michael Douglas) and pop stars have been lured by the beauty of the island and have bought expensive homes there.

Other popular tourist haunts include the Costa del Sol and the Costa Brava, both on the Mediterranean mainland coast. The town of Benidorm epitomises the development that has taken place along these once quiet shores (see page 53). Today Benidorm is full of large hotels, garish bars and nightclubs catering for people who want cheap holiday breaks in the sun. In recent years, however, this type of holiday has become less fashionable, and Spain is under pressure to adapt its resorts to appeal to tourists who want something more than just an inexpensive beach holiday.

MOUNTAINS AND MUSEUMS

There is more to Spain than sun and sandy beaches. Today many tourists come to hike or mountain-bike in the Cordillera Cantabrica or the Pyrenees, or to windsurf at Tarifa, one of the best places in Europe to practise this sport. They may want to sail between the quieter islands in the Mediterranean, to rock-climb on the many cliffs and gorges of the hinterland, or to sightsee and enjoy the good seafood in Galicia. Spain also offers world-class city holidays. Cities like Madrid, Granada, Barcelona and Córdoba offer art galleries, museums, theatre, vibrant nightlife, Roman antiquities and Moorish buildings. There are more than 10,000 castles and other historic monuments to visit across the country, including the Escorial monastery palace, built outside Madrid by King Philip II of Spain in 1584, which has been described as the eighth wonder of the world. The works of artists such as El Greco, Velázquez, Goya, Salvador Dali and Pablo Picasso, and the strange and beautiful architecture of Antoni Gaudí (1852–1926) in Barcelona, attract visitors from all over the world.

The Casa Battlo, one of Antoni Gaudí's highly unusual buildings in Barcelona.

GOLF

Golf is big business in Spain, and many Spanish people play the game for recreation. There are also world class Spanish golf players, such as Sergio García. Golf attracts many thousands of players from all over Europe, especially in the off-season when those from northern countries have difficulty playing on their own courses because the weather is poor. From November to March, groups of club players come to sample the numerous courses across the country and to enjoy the weather of the warmer and drier south. The golf course at Valderrama, near Cádiz, is among the best in Europe and hosts the annual Volvo Masters tournament.

SKIING AND SNOWBOARDING

Spain offers many different venues for skiing, from the Sierra Nevada mountain range near Granada to the various resorts in the Pyrenees and the Cantabrian Mountains along the north coast. Sol y Nieve is the most southerly of all ski resorts in Europe. Its proximity to Granada means that crowds of local people flock there at weekends. In the Pyrenees there are resorts such as Candanchu, Astun and Jaca in Aragon. Jaca is making a bid to hold the 2014 Winter Olympics. In Cataluña there is the Vall de

A golf course in Marbella, southern Spain.

The winter sports of skiing and snowboarding are popular in the high Sierra Nevada, south-east of Granada.

Nuria resort and Baquiesa Beret, the largest ski resort in Spain. One of the few professional Spanish skiers to reach international acclaim in the sport, Paco Fernández Ochoa, won a gold medal in the Winter Olympics for the slalom event. There are several small ski resorts near Madrid. They include Navacerrada and Valdesqui, which are within easy reach of the capital. These resorts tend not to attract skiers from outside the region because the conditions are not reliable, but they are popular among people from Madrid, who use them when the conditions are right.

Half a century of tourism has undoubtedly brought great economic benefit to Spain and its people. But there has been a cost. Huge hotel complexes, casinos, golf courses and beach resorts have swallowed up entire villages and ports along the southern coast. Farming and fishing communities have dwindled as young people have turned away from traditional occupations and sought work in the lucrative tourist trade. Despite this, Spain still has high unemployment – over 11 per cent of the 17 million working population (almost 2 million) are registered as out of work.

CASE STUDY
MINI HOLLYWOOD

Around the desert town of Tabernas in eastern Andalucía, near the coastal city of Almeria, are film sets with names like Fort Apache, where many famous Westerns and other American films have been made. With its dry and treeless landscape, this location presents itself as a convincing stand-in for the deserts of the USA. The sets were built in the 1960s and 1970s for films such as *A Fistful of Dollars*, directed by Italian film-maker Sergio Leone and starring Clint Eastwood. Local people took the roles of Mexican bandits. One of the attractions for the film-makers were the low wages that could be paid at the time to these extras, compared with the fees demanded by US bit-part players. Today, the film sets have become theme parks. Tourists can visit the Wild West saloon bars for a drink and watch mock gunfights and bank raids. Other films shot in the Tabernas Desert include *Patton* and *Indiana Jones and the Last Crusade*.

DAILY LIFE

Senior citizens engrossed in a game of dominoes taking place outside a café in the main square.

During the past 30 years there have been more changes to life in Spain than in any other Western European country. Since the death of General Franco, standards of education and healthcare have improved, and there are better-paid and more varied careers for young people.

EDUCATION

Spain has a modern compulsory and free education system at primary and secondary levels (6 to 16 years old). State education is funded through taxation and administered at a national level by the Ministry of Education, Culture and Sport. About 5.5 per cent of the GDP (gross domestic product) is currently spent on education. In Spain a greater number of 3- to 5-year-olds (70 per cent) attend nursery school than in any other European country. There are more than 16,000 establishments catering for them, with about 250,000 nursery teachers. Primary education is similarly well provided for, with more than 13,000 schools and some 138,000 teachers looking after 2.5 million pupils. Children start secondary school at the age of 12; and there are more than 8,000 schools, 270,000 teachers and 3 million pupils.

HEALTHCARE

Since Spain joined the EU in 1986, its healthcare system has experienced a revolution. It has changed from an under-funded service to one in which successive governments have invested heavily to create a high quality free service. In spite of this, more than six million Spaniards still choose to take out private health insurance. The national health service is paid for through taxation, and amounts to about 7 per cent of Spain's GDP. All towns and cities have at least one hospital or clinic. There are around 800 hospitals throughout Spain, with 163,000 beds, 164,000 doctors and 172,000 nurses. There are also some 12,000 dentists. Each of the 17 main autonomous regions runs its own health service, although the national government monitors overall expenditure and performance.

HEALTH SERVICE PRESSURES

On average, the population of Spain is living longer and there are a greater number of older people in the community. Inevitably, older people need more healthcare than any other age group. In response to the increased demand on healthcare provision, certain services, such as the ambulance service, have been considerably upgraded and now have the latest equipment. Spain has the highest incidence of AIDS in Europe, and treatment for this disease is very costly. Also, under new legislation, immigrant workers from North Africa and Eastern Europe are entitled to healthcare, which is a further cost to the taxpayer. Finally, tourists visiting the country occasionally fall ill and need treatment.

NURSING HOMES

Traditionally in Spain, the elderly are looked after at home. In the recent past it was common for three generations or more to live in the same household. Even today, Spain has the highest average number of people living under one roof in Europe, and the lowest average number of people living alone. However, things are slowly changing. There are a quarter of a million nursing home beds available for the elderly throughout the country. As Spanish society gradually becomes more like that of other European countries, and families begin to favour nursing homes, developers and construction companies have been quick to seize the opportunity to build more of them.

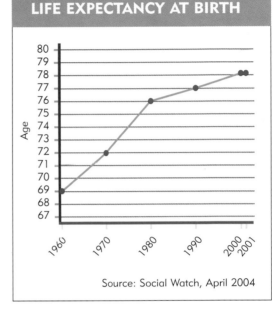

LIFE EXPECTANCY AT BIRTH

Source: Social Watch, April 2004

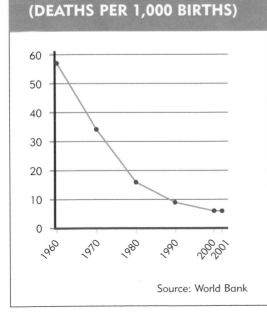

UNDER-FIVE MORTALITY RATE (DEATHS PER 1,000 BIRTHS)

Source: World Bank

Primary school children in their playground in Baena.

COMMUNICATIONS AND THE MEDIA

Spain has embraced modern communications technology. Today there are almost as many mobile phones in use in the country as there are people. In 2003, there were almost 10,000,000 registered Internet users (both home and business) and this number is growing daily. Every town and city has its fair share of Internet cafes, used by people of all ages. Computers are commonplace throughout society – used extensively at work and in the home.

TV AND CENSORSHIP

Spain has more than two hundred television broadcast stations and four times as many radio stations. Many regions, such as Galicia, Cataluña, the Basque Country and Andalucía have their own television stations that broadcast local programmes, often in regional languages. The major cities have their own television stations, too. The first television station was *Television Española*, which started up in 1956. It was controlled by General Franco's government, however, and was therefore heavily censored. After Franco's death, the media in general enjoyed far more freedom as the state drew away from both ownership and interference with the content of programmes.

Today, the Spanish spend more hours in front of the television than almost any other

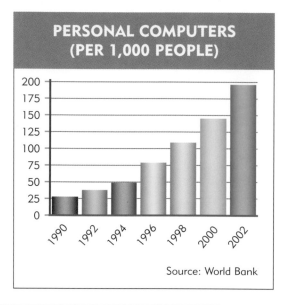

PERSONAL COMPUTERS (PER 1,000 PEOPLE)

Source: World Bank

A busy Internet café in the centre of Granada, used by students, tourists and local people.

Local and national newspapers displayed on a stand outside a kiosk.

TELECOMMUNICATIONS DATA (PER 1,000 PEOPLE)

Mainline phones	506
Mobile phones	824
Internet users	156

Source: World Bank

people in Europe. The most popular national channels include TVE1, a state channel aimed at a very general audience, which has about 20 million viewers each day, and *Canal 5*. Here viewers can see plenty of live football in the season. Popular programmes include numerous soaps that grip the nation. Many of these are imported from South America, Australia, the USA and the UK. Films are also popular entertainment. Many of these are also imported and dubbed into Spanish or subtitled.

FREEDOM OF THE PRESS

Spanish newspapers and journals were only allowed free expression in 1978, the year in which the nation started to throw off the oppressive yoke of the Franco regime. Before this date, the government had heavily censored them, along with all the other media. Censorship of television output remained in place into the 1980s, as a result of the legacy of state ownership of the television channels.

In general, the Spanish are not enthusiastic newspaper readers. It is thought that only one in ten adults buys a daily newspaper. This figure may not accurately reflect the true readership, however, as there is a culture of café-going, where newspapers are often freely available for customers to read. The Spanish are one of the most gregarious peoples in Europe, and they enjoy visiting a bar or café to read the papers or to swap comments on their favourite football team or some unpopular political decision. The most popular newspaper is *El Pais*, which has a circulation of fewer than half a million. It contains good coverage of foreign news, as well as literature and arts events in Spain and listings of what is coming up. Other important daily newspapers are *ABC* and *El Mundo*. *AS* and *Marca* are dedicated to sports, especially football. Spain is also the country that gave the world the best-selling magazine, *Hola* (known as *Hello* magazine in the UK).

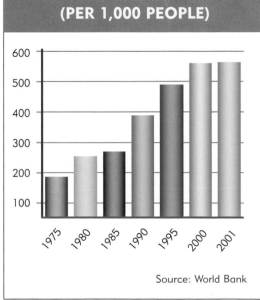

TELEVISION SETS (PER 1,000 PEOPLE)

Source: World Bank

Young men play guitars in the streets. Spanish culture encourages expressive personal displays like this.

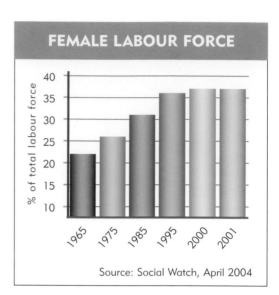

FEMALE LABOUR FORCE

% of total labour force

Source: Social Watch, April 2004

LIFE IN THE CITY

Most Spanish people today choose to live in towns and cities, where they can develop their careers, and enjoy good restaurants and cultural amenities such as museums, theatres, cinemas and concert halls. In the last twenty years or more, as industry and business have grown up around the cities and along the tourist coast, agriculture and the countryside in general have paid the price. People have uprooted themselves and moved to the cities to take jobs. This depopulation of the countryside has caused problems in some remote rural villages. In the province of Aragon in the east of the country, for example, people traditionally worked on small farms. Many members of the younger generation have left the area and entire villages are now populated almost exclusively by older people. The farms themselves have inevitably suffered and a whole way of life is disappearing.

MADRID

Until the middle of the sixteenth century, Madrid was a small, poor farming town in the hot and dusty *Meseta* in the centre of Spain. In 1561, the Spanish king, Philip II, decided he wanted this Castilian town as his new capital and built his palace, the Escorial, on the outskirts. Today, Madrid has a population of over three million. It is a city of culture, with many fine old buildings, great museums and art galleries (for example, the Museo del Prado and the Reina Sofia). However, Madrid also has some of the ugliest suburbs of any major city in Europe – many of them built

The famous Madrid flea market, El Rastro, on a busy weekend with scarcely room to move between the stalls.

under Franco. Madrid came back to life after Franco's death. The regeneration was carried forward by one of Madrid's most famous mayors, Tierro Galvan. He opened the city up to the people, by building parks, for example. He also encouraged a more outward looking attitude and positively encouraged tourists.

Today, Madrid has an international reputation for the arts, for restaurants and *tapas* bars (see pages 23 and 49), and as an exciting place to visit. The centre of the city is the Puerta del Sol, a square vibrant with shops and bars. To the west is the royal residence, the Palacio Real. The wide paths that surround it are popular with locals out for their early evening *paseo* (stroll). Madrid has a botanical garden and numerous parks, including the Campo del Moro behind the palace. During the weekend, the famous flea market of El Rastro is packed with people looking for bargains or simply watching the crowds.

BARCELONA

Spain's second most important city is Barcelona, a major port on the Mediterranean and the capital of Cataluña. Barcelona is a prosperous, noisy, bustling place with a great deal of creative energy and charm. This artistic side of the city is perhaps most obviously expressed in the strange and individualistic architecture of Antoni Gaudí.

CASE STUDY
MUSEU PICASSO

Pablo Picasso (1881–1973) was one of the most important artists of the twentieth century. He was born in Málaga in Andalucía, and lived in Barcelona as a teenager and young man. The museum named after him contains many of his most influential and well-known works of art. It is the biggest tourist attraction in Barcelona.

He trained as an architect in the city and has left as his legacy some of the weirdest buildings in the world – such as the church of Sagrada Familia or the smaller Casa Vicens.

There is great rivalry between Barcelona and Madrid. This is evident in the competition that exists between their respective football teams, Real Madrid and FC Barcelona.

The Sagrada Familia, the world-famous cathedral designed by Antoni Gaudí in Barcelona.

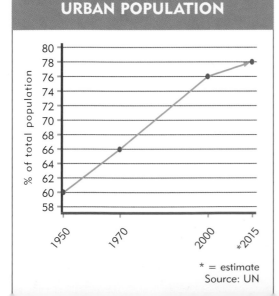

URBAN POPULATION

% of total population

80
78
76
74
72
70
68
66
64
62
60
58

1950   1970   2000   *2015

* = estimate
Source: UN

LIFE IN RURAL SPAIN

The Spanish countryside is dotted with run-down, old-fashioned small farms that have not moved into the twenty-first century. Farmers can still be seen using the donkey and cart to move small amounts of produce around. But Spain also has many large scale, modern and profitable farms, many of which employ cheap labour from North Africa or Eastern Europe. The smaller farms are being priced out of the market and bought up by larger ones, looking to become larger still. Better roads and communications mean that agricultural produce can reach market far quicker than it used to, even if the market is a supermarket in a town or city in another EU country. Distribution of goods has become a priority for Spanish agriculture.

FOREIGN INVASION

Spain's agreeable climate and low property prices mean that there has been an influx of foreigners (mostly other Europeans) buying up and renovating old farms in the countryside. As a result, property prices are now rising faster in Spain than in any other country in Europe. Many foreign buyers have headed for Andalucía, away from the crowded beaches, but close enough to make day trips to the sea. They include young couples looking for a holiday home or for a house in which to live permanently and bring up a family. Other buyers include the recently retired or those who have decided to start a rural holiday business, renting accommodation to tourists, for example. Some foreign settlers just want to drop out altogether, following a pattern

A prosperous farm with newly renovated buildings and equipped with a modern swimming pool.

that was set in the 1960s, when locations such as Mallorca and Andalucía attracted American and European hippies and travellers looking for an alternative way of life.

RURAL DEVELOPMENT

In the past, Spanish rural villages were isolated, enclosed places and people tended to stay close to home. Today, many of these villages are undergoing enormous changes. With help from EU funding for regional development, Spanish developers have built new houses on the outskirts. The population is generally more mobile than it used to be and there has been a dramatic rise in the number of cars. Inevitably, village communities have changed as a consequence.

A small, traditional village on the edge of the Tabernas Desert in southern Spain.

A woman inside her home built in caves at Guadix in Andalucía.

The government is also providing grants to people who want to buy and renovate old buildings, especially if they plan to start a business. This is part of the regeneration schemes set up to help repopulate and re-stimulate the economies of rural regions. New roads are being built in these regions to give easier access to nearby large towns and cities. Professional people with jobs and homes in urban areas now have the opportunity to buy a weekend rural retreat.

CASE STUDY
SPAIN ABROAD

Many Spanish people have chosen to live abroad. A good number of them have settled down with a partner from another country, or have set up a business abroad. The USA and Spanish-speaking South American countries are popular destinations. Now that EU citizens can travel and find work anywhere within Europe, many Spaniards are choosing to settle in other European countries too. Spanish restaurants usually attract good custom in foreign towns and cities. All the major cities of Europe and North America have their fair share of *tapas* bars, for example. These traditional bars serving small portions of food to accompany alcoholic drinks have become a symbol of Spain.

ENVIRONMENT AND WILDLIFE

Smog lies heavily over the city of Granada. Pollution from vehicles and industry is a common problem in urban areas across the country.

For many decades, Spain's natural environment has been neglected. During the latter part of the twentieth century, the country's rapid economic growth meant that businesses and government focused on building hotels for tourists, developing the infrastructure (roads, railways and airports) and giving incentives to companies to generate income and employment. As a result, the landscape in some parts of the country has suffered. The problems include soil erosion, the expansion of deserts (desertification) and barren land, deforestation, polluted rivers and seas, ugly buildings, noisy streets in once quiet towns, and poor air quality in the inner cities.

NATIONAL PARKS

Spain still has vast regions of wild landscape. It is one of the few countries in Western Europe in which wolves roam wild. Other rare animals include the black vulture, colourful lizards, ibex (a type of wild goat), chamois, the Iberian lynx (a member of the wild cat family), and the eagle owl (Europe's largest owl).

There are more than two hundred Spanish nature reserves, small areas protected by law.

The first national park was created in 1918 and there are now twelve altogether. These parks are much larger than the nature reserves and the laws governing them are stricter. Animals in the parks are protected from hunting and the land is protected from being developed. Regional government is responsible for the national parks and oversees and enforces the laws that protect them.

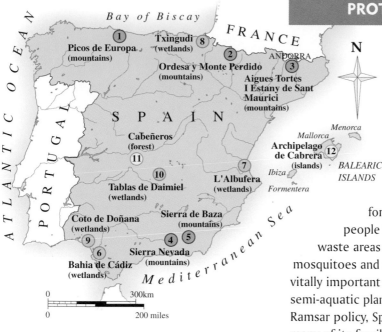

13. **Garajanay** (forest)
14. **Caldera de Taburiente** (volcano)
15. **Teide** (volcano)
16. **Timafaya** (volcano)

CANARY ISLANDS

Lanzarote 16
La Palma *Fuerteventura*
14 *Tenerife*
15
13 *Gran*
Canaria

BALEARIC ISLANDS

Bay of Biscay

FRANCE

ATLANTIC OCEAN

PORTUGAL

S P A I N

ANDORRA

1

Picos de Europa
(mountains)

Txingudi 8
(wetlands)

Ordesa y Monte Perdido
(mountains)

2

3

Aigues Tortes I Estany de Sant Maurici
(mountains)

7

Menorca
Mallorca

Archipelago de Cabrera
(islands)

12

Ibiza

Formentera

Cabeñeros
(forest)

11

10

Tablas de Daimiel
(wetlands)

L'Albufera
(wetlands)

Coto de Doñana
(wetlands)

9

Sierra de Baza
(mountains)

4 5

6

Sierra Nevada
(mountains)

Bahía de Cádiz
(wetlands)

Mediterranean Sea

0   300km
0   200 miles

and develop the land – either for building or farming. Some people believe that wetlands are waste areas and a breeding ground for mosquitoes and malaria. But these places are vitally important for birds, fish and aquatic or semi-aquatic plant species. In adopting the Ramsar policy, Spain is ensuring a future for many of its fragile wetland regions.

RAMSAR

The Ramsar Convention protects wetlands and has responsibility for thousands of sites all over the world. In Spain alone there are 49 Ramsar sites. The most important is the Doñana National Park. Other wetland sites range from the small (for example, the Txingudi coastal marshes covering 128 hectares on the border with France) to the large (for example, the Bahía de Cádiz, a 10,000-hectare site of Atlantic coastal marshland, home to many wintering and migrating birds). Wetlands have been under attack from people who want to dry them out

ENFORCING THE LAW

In the Sierra de Baza Nature Park, 14,000 trees were felled illegally. The Spanish nature conservation service, *Seprona*, reported the damage done to the trees and emphasised that this wholesale removal of tree cover would endanger local animals and other vegetation by destroying the habitat. When they can, the local authorities prosecute people who damage the environment illegally, but they often find it difficult to detect who has carried out the crime. Cases such as the Sierra de Baza event are reported every year in Spain.

A sign welcoming people to the Doñana National Park.

Barren and burnt land: desertification is a major problem in Spain.

WATER WARS

Tourists are keen to visit the hotter and drier regions of Spain, provided that they are reasonably close to the sea. As facilities have been developed to accommodate the tourists, so the struggle over who controls and ultimately gets the precious water in these regions has reached crisis point. Golf courses need lots of water to keep the grass green and healthy for the players. Restaurants and hotels need water for drinking, cooking, washing and cleaning. In areas where water is in short supply, the local inhabitants, the poorer farmers, have lost out. For example, Cataluña in eastern Spain has a long coastline that has been highly developed for the tourist trade. The government has poured money into developing the region. The relatively poor agricultural region of Aragon borders Cataluña. Water has been taken from Aragon to meet the needs of the tourists who come to the Cataluñan coast.

A water purification plant. Careful water storage and use is important in a country as hot and dry as Spain.

One major problem Spanish fishermen face today is depleted stocks of fish and seafood. The reason for this is over-fishing. Quite simply, too many fish have been taken from the fishing grounds of Galicia. Although the Atlantic Ocean is vast, it is not limitless. Today, many of the 20,000 registered fishing vessels in Galicia must sail as far afield as the coasts of Iceland and Canada to obtain their catch. This problem is not unique to Galicia. European waters in general are suffering from over-fishing. A favourite Spanish food is salted cod (*bacalao*). Atlantic cod has been among the worst affected of all fish, and stocks are extremely low.

EFFECTS OF TOURISM

Tourism has not traditionally been a friend to the environment. It is an industry that has seen the wholesale and unregulated development of high-rise hotels, golf courses that suck up precious water from the landscape, and concrete apartments. As a result of poor planning and lack of investment, sewage and other forms of pollution have in the past poured unchecked into the Mediterranean. However, many tourists have changed their habits in recent years. More people are looking for holidays that suit their individual tastes, rather than a beach holiday at some large resort. Tourists now choose from a range of options, including cultural city breaks, wine-tasting journeys through the vineyards of Spain's 57 wine-producing regions, or exciting outdoor adventures, such as rock-climbing in the El Chorro gorge in southern Spain or taking to the mountain trails on foot or mountain bike. There is more literature available to inform the tourist on

The seafront at Benidorm is lined with high-rise hotels and apartment blocks for holidaymakers.

what is available in all the regions. These more educated tourists will often make choices based on certain environmental considerations. For example, they may choose to stay in resorts or regions that have 'green' strategies for their area.

In recent years the Spanish tourist authorities seem to have responded to these subtle but important changes in the market. They have attempted to attract the more discerning tourist, by building smaller and more exclusive hotels in regions where once the mass market dominated. Eco-tourism has also captured the attention of policy-makers and business people. People are far more aware today of the impact they have on the environments they live in and choose to visit. People are now far more willing to enjoy holidays in Spain in ways that work with, rather than against, the environment.

Cyclists gather in a city park in preparation for a Sunday workout. Cycling is an environmentally friendly way of exercising and having fun, and cycling holidays are becoming increasingly popular in Spain.

Will young art students such as these face problems of finding jobs and affording homes in the future?

In the past half century, Spain has moved from an agriculturally based country to a modern industrial nation. The Spanish people have generally become more prosperous, but economic progress has come at a price. Social and economic change has led to increased pressures on family life, the traditional cornerstone of Spanish society. In general, couples are producing fewer babies and fewer families are now caring for their older relatives. This suggests that men and women are pursuing their careers at the expense of their families.

UNEMPLOYMENT

Unemployment remains a problem: in 1994 it was 24 per cent, almost a quarter of the entire workforce, today it is over 11 per cent and still among the highest in Western Europe. Spain's economic and national wealth is about 20 per cent lower than that of countries such as Germany, the UK and France. One of the biggest social problems facing the Spanish government today is how to bridge the gap between average income and the cost of buying or renting a house. For example, from 1987 to 1990 the cost of housing increased by around 65 per cent, while incomes increased

by an average of only 28 per cent. Many young people cannot now afford to buy or rent properties in their own country, where house prices have increased beyond wages. This is partly the result of the high numbers of foreign investors (from Germany, the UK and the Scandinavian countries in particular) buying homes in Spain. Young people cannot afford to leave home, which means they postpone getting married. The average age at which people marry today is about 27 years, much older than that of previous generations.

Health and education are also important issues for the twenty-first century. While there has been a lot of growth and improvement in the health service, the problem of how to continue paying for it and developing it forms the basis for ongoing political debate. There have also been improvements in education, and around 97 per cent of the population can now read and write. Schools are well funded, and many teenagers go on to higher, post-compulsory education.

ENVIRONMENT ISSUES

When Spain joined the EU it was forced to tighten up its environmental laws. In spite of this, industrial and tourist developments appear to have continued unhindered. In some places these have created pollution problems, with instances of raw sewage and chemical waste being discharged into the water supply and the Mediterranean Sea. Deforestation has continued, as has desertification, which still gives cause for concern in the dry hinterland of Andalucía. Spain is committed to continued improvements in its environmental standards, meeting European Union laws and directives.

A recently built small hospital on the edge of a thriving Spanish town.

However, it also plans to maintain the growth of its economy, to push ahead with road-building and house construction plans, and to enable industry and business to flourish. Just how these programmes will develop alongside one another remains to be seen.

A man sleeps rough on the streets of Madrid. Homelessness and drug addiction are significant problems in Spain today.

TERRITORIAL MATTERS

Gibraltar is a promontory at the tip of Spain. In 1704 it was captured by the British Navy and has remained in effect a British colony ever since. The Spanish government has disputed the right of the British to run Gibraltar on many occasions, but without success. In 2003, a referendum was held for the people living in Gibraltar and they voted overwhelmingly to remain under British rule.

Where Spain's interests in North Africa are concerned, the situation is reversed. Morocco disputes the right of Spain to govern the enclaves of Ceuta and Melilla on the North African coast. Morocco also argues that Spain should surrender the governance of the tiny islands of Peñon de Velez de la Gomera, Peñon de Alhucemas and Islas Chaforinas. Disputes such as these do nothing to enhance cooperation between nations, but it is difficult to see a solution that would be acceptable to all parties.

TERRORISM

In March 2004, Rodriguez Zapatero was elected president of Spain following the terrorist attack near Madrid that killed many people. The Spanish authorities initially assumed that the attack was the work of ETA. But it is thought to have been carried out by Islamic terrorists, in protest against Spain's support for the US invasion of Iraq. Through its history (700 years of Muslim rule) and proximity to North Africa (a few kilometres across the Mediterranean at its closest point), Spain has strong links with the Muslim world and with Morocco in particular. This often tense relationship has been made even more difficult under present circumstances. Radical Muslims in the Middle East, North Africa and Europe have turned to terrorism or aiding terrorists. Western countries are on high alert, with security services working to identify the troublemakers both in their own communities and among the global travelling community.

A view from Spain across a short stretch of sea to Morocco on the North African coast.

DRUGS AND IMMIGRATION

In common with the USA and other Western European countries, Spain has a problem with drugs among the younger members of its population. Spain's historical links and its geographical position make it a European gateway for drugs traffickers. Drugs enter Spain from two main sources – Latin America and Africa. Cocaine arrives from Latin America, with which Spain has strong current and historical ties; and hashish is smuggled in from Morocco, North Africa. The drugs find a local market in Spain itself, but many are also smuggled from Spain into other European countries.

Spain's proximity to North Africa presents it with another major problem – that of illegal immigration. The coast of Morocco is a mere 15km away across the Strait of Gibraltar. Every year, many hundreds of North African people are caught attempting to enter Spain illegally by this route and inevitably some get through. It is estimated that there are at least 500,000 illegal immigrants in Spain, though the real figure could be higher.

SPAIN AND THE EU

In spite of the problems Spain faces, her people remain optimistic. Spain has been the first nation to vote to ratify the new EU constitution. Since the mid-1980s, the EU has given the Spanish economy so much help that there is a huge sense of loyalty among the population. This is a positive force within society, enhanced by economic growth and a dramatic decline in unemployment (though this is still high). Improved transport links to other EU countries mean that movement of goods has improved. Logistics (the business of efficient movement of goods) is a major growth area in the Spanish economy, and a sure indication of the importance of trade. Today Spain appears to face a bright future within the wider European community.

Illegal immigrants from Morocco are led away after being caught by Spanish police near Tarifa.

European Union money has made a big difference in urban regeneration in Spain over the past decade.

GLOSSARY

AIDS Acquired Immune Deficiency Syndrome. An illness caused by the HIV virus that attacks the human immune system.

Alhambra A Moorish word that means 'Red Fort'. It describes the colour of the rock used in the building.

Altitude The height above sea level of any particular place or natural feature.

Aqueduct A channel built to carry water from a river or lake.

Capitalism An economic system that relies on private companies and businesses run for profit in a competitive environment to control the market.

Castanets Two hollowed pieces of hard wood, joined by cord and held in the hand. They are used to make a clicking sound, which helps to keep the rhythm of the flamenco dancers.

Civil war A war in which a country is at war with itself. The Spanish Civil War was fought between the right-wing forces of General Franco (which stood for traditional values of monarchy, the army and the Church) and their left-wing opposition.

Deforestation The removal from the landscape of the natural tree cover by felling and logging, for timber or land to farm. Deforestation usually leads to environmental problems, such as erosion.

Delta A usually triangular shaped landform created by a river when it deposits sand and silt upon entering a sea or lake.

Enclave Territory owned by one country but cut off from it and surrounded by another country.

Erosion The removal of soil and wearing away of rocks by the processes of water (in the form of rain, ice, rivers or waves of the sea) and wind.

European Union The name given to the group of European countries that have signed treaties to work together for mutual financial, economic, social and political advancement.

Falangist Party The right-wing political party of General Franco. Franco was assisted by Hitler and Mussolini during the Spanish Civil War.

Fossil fuels Coal, oil and gas are all fossil fuels. They are made from the fossilised remains of plants and other organisms that lived millions of years ago.

GDP (Gross Domestic Product) The total value of all the goods and services produced by a country in a single year.

Glacier A river of ice, usually found in the mountains or close to the Arctic or Antarctic.

GNI (Gross National Income) The total value of all the goods and services produced by a country along with all its income from overseas, in a single year.

Greenhouse gases Gases given off by industry and cars that are thought to contribute to the heating up of the world. The main gases are carbon dioxide (CO_2) and methane.

HEP (hydroelectric power) Electricity generated by utilising the force of moving water (for example, in a fast-flowing river, or flowing through a dam).

Heritage Valuable objects, money, property, ancient monuments and cultural traditions passed down from generation to generation.

Immigrant A person who goes to live in a country other than his or her country of origin.

Industrial Revolution A period in British history that started at the end of the eighteenth century. Machinery was invented to speed up the production of wool and cotton cloth and other processes. The machines were driven by coal furnaces and steam power. The industrial process spread to other countries, such as Germany and the USA, in the nineteenth century.

Irrigation Watering the land by using channels, drip or sprinkler systems.

Islam The religion of the Moorish people who conquered much of Spain in the eighth century and who ruled until the fifteenth century. Also called Muslims, they are followers of the Prophet Muhammad.

Migrants People who have moved from the country in which they were born to live in another country.

Militant The use of violence, or a person who uses violence, to achieve a political outcome.

Peninsula A geographical term that describes an area of land surrounded on three sides by the sea.

Plateau A geographical word that means a high, flat area of land.

Promontory A high point of land that juts out into the sea.

GLOSSARY

Rain shadow The dry region behind a mountain range. Mountains are usually wet places. They force the air to rise and form clouds. Rain falls on them but the region behind the mountain receives very little rain.

Ramsar A city in Iran where in 1971 scientists and environmentalists met to discuss how best to protect the world's wetlands from further drainage and pollution. They designated wetlands of great importance Ramsar sites. These became protected areas.

Referendum The process by which the people are asked their opinion on a single question by the government. The decision is determined by popular vote.

Service industry Includes industries that provide services, such as public transport, tourism, communications and healthcare.

Silt Tiny particles of mud and rock gathered by a river as it travels from the mountains to the sea. Silt settles when the river slows down at the end of its journey. It is a good growing medium because it is very fertile.

Smog Pollution in the air over a town or city that becomes thick enough to see. The word comes from the combination of the two words 'smoke' and 'fog'.

Temperate A climate that generally avoids extremes of temperature or weather, but is characterised by being mild.

United Nations An international organisation set up in 1945 to promote world peace, cooperation between nations and security in the world. Its headquarters are in New York City, USA.

Urbanisation The process of expansion of towns and cities.

FURTHER INFORMATION

BOOKS TO READ:
NON-FICTION:

Spain: Eyewitness Travel Guides (Dorling Kindersley Ltd, 2004) Highly illustrated travel guide for all ages.

Lonely Planet Guide: Spain by Damien Simonis and others (Lonely Planet Publications, 4th edition 2003) Budget travel guide for travellers of all ages.

The Rough Guide: Spain by Mark Ellingham and John Fisher (Rough Guides, 2001) Budget travel guide for travellers of all ages.

A Traveller's History of Spain by Juan Lalaguna (The Windrush Press, 1990) A concise history of Spain up to the 1980s.

Duende: A Journey in Search of Flamenco by Jason Webster (Black Swan, 2003) A personal journey to discover the roots of flamenco.

Andalus: Unlocking the Secrets of Moorish Spain by Jason Webster (Doubleday, 2004).

FICTION:

Don Quixote by Miguel de Cervantes, translated by John Rutherford (Penguin Classics, 2001) First published in 1605, this book has remained the classic novel from Spanish literature.

WEBSITES:

The CIA World Factbook
www.cia.gov/cia/publications/factbook/geos/sp.html
The CIA World Factbook online, with facts and analysis of all the world's countries.

WWF
www.wwf.org
The website of WWF. Click on the link for Spain.

The Ramsar Convention on Wetlands
www.ramsar.org
The site of the Ramsar Convention, with lots of information on Spanish wetlands, including the Coto de Doñana.

Spanish Embassy
http://.spain.embassyhomepage.com
The official website of the Spanish Embassy.

Spanish Tourism
www.tourspain.es
The website of the Spanish tourist board.

INDEX

A small, beautiful square in the ancient city of Córdoba.